Let's Cook

Nicola Graimes

MARKS &
SPENCER

Marks and Spencer p.l.c.
PO Box 3339
Chester CH99 9QS

shop online
www.marksandspencer.com

ISBN: 978-1-84805-606-0

Printed in China

Written by Nicola Graimes
Photography by Mike Cooper
Food styling by Lincoln Jefferson
Designed by Seamonster Design

With a special thank you to Ruby, Harvey, Jacob, Matthew, Asia, Gabrielle, Giselle, Nikki and Chris.

The views expressed in this book are those of the author but they are general views only and readers are urged to consult a relevant and qualified specialist for individual advice in particular situations. Marks and Spencer p.l.c. and Exclusive Editions Limited hereby exclude all liability to the extent permitted by law for any errors or omissions in this book and for any loss, damage or expense (whether direct or indirect) suffered by a third party relying on any information contained in this book.

Notes for the Reader
This book uses both metric and imperial measurements. Follow the same units of measurement throughout; do not mix metric and imperial. All spoon measurements are level: teaspoons are assumed to be 5 ml, and tablespoons are assumed to be 15 ml. Unless otherwise stated, milk is assumed to be full fat, eggs and individual vegetables are medium, and pepper is freshly ground black pepper.

The times given are an approximate guide only. Preparation times differ according to the techniques used by different people and the cooking times may also vary from those given. Optional ingredients, variations or serving suggestions have not been included in the calculations.

Recipes using raw or very lightly cooked eggs should be avoided by infants, the elderly, pregnant women, convalescents and anyone suffering from an illness. Pregnant and breastfeeding women are advised to avoid eating peanuts and peanut products. Sufferers from nut allergies should be aware that some of the ready-made ingredients used in the recipes in this book may contain nuts. Always check the packaging before use.

Contents

Cooking together................................ 4

Cooking tips..................................... 5

How to… 6

Essential equipment.......................... 7

Recipe record chart 8

Great start.................................... 12

Super snacks 24

Meals in minutes............................. 36

Sweet treats.................................. 48

Cooking words 62

Index 64

Cooking together

Cooking is fun and it's even more fun if you can do it with someone else. All the recipes in this book have been created for you – the "head chef" – to cook with an adult – "kitchen assistant" – with lots of delicious results. Cooking is all about enjoyment, learning and experimenting and there are plenty of ideas here for you to try, from breakfasts and lunches to suppers and puddings. You can make a note of your cooking successes in the Recipe Record Chart on page 8 – get your family and friends to give you marks out of 10!

Before you start...

There are a few guidelines and important rules to remember when you are cooking. The following tips will make sure your recipes taste great and work every time.

1 Read the recipe before you start: try to get all your ingredients ready and make sure you have the equipment listed.

2 Wash your hands before you start cooking, put an apron on to protect your clothes and tie your hair back if it is long.

3 For successful results, take care when weighing and measuring your ingredients. Weigh dry ingredients on kitchen scales and use a measuring jug or spoon for liquids.

Cooking tips

Using the recipes

The recipes in this book are graded with stars, meaning that some are more difficult than others:

★ = easy

★ ★ = medium

★ ★ ★ = more difficult

The recipes also have symbols to help you. Look out for:

⬡ Serves/Makes

◉ Preparation time

◗ Cooking time

Safe cooking!

- Always ask an adult first before starting to cook and take extra care when handling anything hot, sharp or electrical.

- Always wear oven gloves when handling hot trays, tins and dishes.

- When stirring food in a pan, hold the handle firmly to keep it steady.

- Turn pan handles to the side, away from the heat, so they aren't accidentally knocked off the hob.

- Wipe up any spills on the floor to prevent slipping.

- Do not walk around the kitchen with a sharp knife in your hand.

- Remember to switch off the hob, cooker or oven when you have finished cooking.

Clean up and tidy

- Always wash your hands before you start to cook and after handling raw meat and fish.

- Use separate chopping boards for vegetables and meat. If this is not possible, make sure they are washed thoroughly in between uses.

- Store raw and cooked food separately in the fridge.

- Make sure that the ingredients you use have not passed their "use-by" date.

- Wipe down work surfaces after use and make sure everything is clean and tidy.

If you see the ❶ symbol, it means you need to ask an adult to help you. This could be because a hot oven, hob, electrical appliance, sharp knives or scissors are involved in the recipe preparation.

How to...

Here are some useful cookery words and terms:

Grating cheese

Hold the cheese against a grater and rub it up and down over the large holes to make coarse shreds – mind your fingers.

Separating eggs

Crack the egg, pull open the shell with your fingers and let it plop into a bowl. Put an eggcup over the yolk and pour the white into another bowl.

Rubbing in

When making pastry, mix or rub the fat into the flour with your fingertips until the mixture resembles fine breadcrumbs.

Rolling out pastry

Lightly flour the surface and rolling pin then roll out the pastry away from you in gentle movements, turning it occasionally, until it makes a thin sheet.

Whipping

To add air to cream or egg whites, beat them with a whisk until they firm up and form peaks.

Creaming

To add air to cakes, beat the butter and sugar together with a whisk or wooden spoon until they are light and creamy in texture.

Melting chocolate

Put the bowl of chocolate pieces over a pan of gently simmering water – make sure the bowl does not touch the water – until melted.

Cooking pasta/noodles

Put the pasta/noodles in a large pan of boiling salted water. Cook the pasta/noodles in the boiling water, stirring occasionally, until just tender.

Essential equipment

1 saucepans
2 colander
3 cake tin
4 bun tin
5 baking sheet
6 mixing bowl

7 sieve
8 measuring jug
9 lemon squeezer
10 rolling pin
11 oven gloves
12 cooling rack

1 electric blender
2 weighing scales
3 food processor
4 grater
5 tongs
6 electric hand mixer

7 beaters
8 freezer box
9 electric hand blender
10 balloon whisk

1 measuring cups
2 pastry brush
3 flour shaker
4 plastic spatula
5 slotted spoon
6 fish slice
7 scissors
8 sharp knives

9 chopping board
10 garlic crusher
11 pastry cutter
12 vegetable peeler
13 wooden skewers
14 wooden spoon
15 wooden spatula

Recipe record chart

use your wipe-clean pen to fill these in

Recipe	Date cooked	Who for?	Marks out of 10

Recipe record chart

Recipe	Date cooked	who for?	Marks out of 10

Recipe record chart

Recipe	Date cooked	Who for?	Marks out of 10

Recipe record chart

Recipe	Date cooked	Who for?	Marks out of 10

Great start

Breakfast is one of the most important meals as it helps to give your body lots of energy for the day ahead. Ask your mum, dad or adult carer to help you treat the rest of the family to one of these delicious ways to start the day – there's plenty to choose from, such as a rich and creamy smoothie, crunchy honey-oat cereal, scrummy American-style pancakes and, for a weekend treat, a big fry-up.

Sunrise crush and Going bananas ★

Bring a ray of sunshine to your day with these tropical juices that are brimming with goodness. If making juice in a blender, you may want to press it through a sieve to make it smooth.

Serves 4

prep: 10 minutes

cooking: none

What you need:

Sunrise crush
1 medium ripe pineapple
5 oranges, halved
ice cubes, to serve

Going bananas
1 large ripe mango
4 bananas, peeled and cut into chunks
400ml natural thick yogurt
400ml coconut milk

Equipment:

- sharp knife
- chopping board
- electric juicer, blender or food processor
- mixing bowl
- large jug
- dessert spoon

Job 1: ❗

To make 'Sunrise crush', slice off the bottom of the pineapple and stand it upright on a board. Remove the spiky skin then cut into six long pieces.

Job 2: ❗

Purée the pineapple in the electric juicer, blender or food processor.

Job 3:

Squeeze the oranges, then mix the orange and pineapple juices together in a jug. Pour the juice into 4 glasses. Top with ice cubes.

Job 1: ❗

To make 'Going bananas', cut both sides of the mango away from the stone in the middle. Scoop out the flesh with a spoon.

Job 2: ❗

Slice the bananas into chunks and place in the electric juicer, blender or food processor with the mango, yogurt and coconut milk. Put on the lid.

Job 3:

Blend until smooth and frothy then pour the smoothie into 4 glasses. Serve with straws.

marks out of 10

10=yummylicious **9**=truly scrumptious
8=de-lovely **7**=delicious
6=tasty **5**=Mmmmmmm
4=mouth-watering **3**=just nice
2=good **1**=ok

. . . . ✓

15

Perfect porridge ★★

Just the thing to warm you up on a cold winter's morning, this creamy porridge is topped with a cinnamon apple purée, maple syrup and a sprinkling of pecan nuts.

Serves 4

prep: 15 minutes

cooking: 15 minutes

what you need:

200g whole porridge oats

800ml milk

800ml water

8 pecan nuts, to serve (optional)

maple syrup, to serve

Cinnamon apple purée:

4 apples

1 tsp lemon juice

175ml water

½-1 tsp ground cinnamon

Equipment:

• vegetable peeler

• sharp knife

• chopping board

• fork

• small and large saucepans with lids

• large spoon

Job 1:

To make the purée, remove the skin from the apples using a vegetable peeler. Cut the apple into quarters, remove the core then cut into small pieces.

Job 2:

Put the apples, lemon juice, water and cinnamon in a small saucepan. Cover and simmer for 15 minutes until the apples are soft.

Job 3:

While the apple mixture is cooking, put the oats in a large saucepan with the milk and water; bring to the boil.

Job 4:

When the oat mixture is bubbling, reduce the heat to low; half cover the pan with a lid and simmer for 8 minutes, stirring frequently.

Job 5:

Mash the apple with a fork until mushy. Spoon the creamy porridge into 4 bowls then top each one with apple purée.

Job 6:

Add the pecans, if using, and drizzle over the maple syrup. Try arranging the nuts and syrup in a fun pattern, as shown on page 16.

marks out of 10

10=yummylicious 9=truly scrumptious
8=de-lovely 7=delicious
6=tasty 5=Mmmmmmm
4=mouth-watering 3=just nice
2=good 1=ok

. . . .

Golden nuggets ★★

This golden, crunchy breakfast cereal will give you plenty of energy. It's great served with milk or yogurt and topped with your favourite fresh fruit.

Makes about
10 portions

prep: 15 minutes

cooking:
28 minutes

What you need:

65g whole blanched almonds
200g whole porridge oats
55g sesame seeds
55g sunflower seeds
40g pumpkin seeds
3 tbsp sunflower oil
8 tbsp clear honey
65g shelled walnuts, roughly broken
100g raisins

To serve:

your favourite fresh fruit, such as
   raspberries or sliced strawberries,
   bananas or nectarines
milk or natural yogurt

Equipment:

• large mixing bowl

• wooden spoon

• small saucepan

• 2 baking sheets

Job 1: ⚠️

Turn the oven on to 140°C/275°F/Gas Mark 1. Put the almonds, oats and seeds in a large mixing bowl.

Job 2: ⚠️

Put the oil and honey in a small saucepan and, over a medium heat, stir until melted and mixed together.

Job 3:

Pour the honey mixture into the mixing bowl and stir well with a wooden spoon until the nuts, oats and seeds are coated.

Job 4: ⚠️

Spoon the oat mixture onto 2 baking sheets in an even layer and bake for 15 minutes; then mix in the walnuts.

Job 5: ⚠️

Cook the oat mixture for another 10 minutes until golden. (The mixture will become crisp as it cools.)

Job 6:

Put the cereal in a mixing bowl and stir in the raisins; leave to cool. Serve with milk or yogurt and top with fruit.

marks out of 10

10=yummylicious **9**=truly scrumptious
8=de-lovely **7**=delicious
6=tasty **5**=Mmmmmmm
4=mouth-watering **3**=just nice
2=good **1**=ok

. . . . ✓

19

Flipping good ★★

Your family and friends will love these light American-style pancakes – they're so moreish that they'll disappear in seconds! They make a great teatime treat too.

Makes 16

prep: 10 minutes

cooking:
20 minutes

What you need:

150g self-raising flour

2 tbsp caster sugar

1 large egg, lightly beaten

175ml milk

3 tbsp thick natural yogurt, plus extra to serve

2 tbsp unsalted butter, for frying

275g frozen mixed summer fruits, defrosted

maple syrup, to serve

Equipment:

• sieve

• large mixing bowl

• wooden spoon

• jug

• large non-stick frying pan

• palette knife

Job 1:

Sift the flour into a mixing bowl. Stir in the sugar and make a dip in the centre. Mix together the egg and milk in a jug.

Job 2:

Pour the milk mixture into the flour. Add the yogurt and stir with a wooden spoon until you have a smooth batter.

Job 3: (!)

Melt a quarter of the butter in a frying pan. Add 3 spoonfuls of batter to make 3 pancakes, each one about 6cm diameter.

Job 4: (!)

Cook for 2 minutes until bubbles appear on the top and the underneath is golden. Flip each pancake over with a palette knife and cook for another minute.

Job 5: (!)

Repeat with the rest of the batter to make about 16 pancakes. Add a little more butter when the pan looks dry.

Job 6:

Serve the pancakes with a large spoonful of fruit and yogurt and drizzle over the maple syrup.

marks out of 10

10=yummylicious **9**=truly scrumptious
8=de-lovely **7**=delicious
6=tasty **5**=Mmmmmmm
4=mouth-watering **3**=just nice
2=good **1**=ok

. . . .

21

Big breakfast★★

Treat your family to a slap-up weekend breakfast or brunch with this hearty meal of egg, bacon, potato cakes and tomatoes.

Serves 4

prep: 15 minutes

cooking:
20 minutes

What you need:

450g large potatoes, peeled

5 eggs

3 tbsp plain flour

3 tbsp sunflower oil

8 rashers bacon

6 cherry tomatoes, halved, to serve

salt and pepper

Equipment:

- sharp knife
- chopping board
- grater
- mixing bowl
- large frying pan
- fish slice or spatula
- kitchen paper
- small bowl

Job 1:

Grate the potatoes, rinse in a sieve then lay them on a tea towel. Gather up the sides and squeeze to remove any water.

Job 2: (!)

Turn on the grill to medium–high. Put the potatoes in a bowl with 1 beaten egg and flour; season and stir.

Job 3: (!)

Heat 2 tbsp of the oil in a frying pan. Take a handful of the potato mixture and form into rounds, about 7cm across.

Job 4: (!)

Put 3 potato cakes in the pan and cook each side for about 5 minutes until golden; drain on kitchen paper and make 3 more.

Job 5: (!)

Meanwhile, grill the bacon for about 8 minutes, turning once, until crisp. Grill the tomatoes either side for a few minutes. Crack an egg into a bowl then slide into the pan.

Job 6: (!)

Repeat with the rest of the eggs and cook for 5 minutes until the white is set. Serve with the bacon, potato cakes and tomatoes.

marks out of 10

10=yummylicious **9**=truly scrumptious
8=de-lovely **7**=delicious
6=tasty **5**=Mmmmmmm
4=mouth-watering **3**=just nice
2=good **1**=ok

. . . . ✓

Super snacks

Feeling peckish? Ask your kitchen assistant to help you make these tasty tummy fillers. There are ideas for all kinds of occasions, from a movie night at home, to party treats and lunchbox fillers. Some of these recipes would also make a great lunch served with a salad or a selection of crunchy vegetable sticks.

Roll up, roll up! ★

This yummy roll is extra special as it has a secret layer inside,
filled with delicious pesto.

Makes 1

prep: 10 minutes

cooking: none

What you need:

1 large crusty roll
1 tbsp mayonnaise
1 tsp green pesto
2 slices ham or cooked chicken
2 crisp lettuce leaves
30g cheese, cut into thin slices
4 thin, round slices cucumber

Equipment:

- sharp knife
- chopping board
- spoon
- bowl
- cling film

Job 1: ❗

Slice off the top of the roll to form a lid and use a spoon to scoop out the soft bread from the inside to make a hollow.

Job 2:

Mix together the mayonnaise and pesto in a bowl and spread it all over the inside of the roll and the lid.

Job 3:

Fold one of the slices of ham or chicken, then place it in the bottom of the roll. Top with the lettuce leaves.

Job 4:

Next, add the remaining slice of ham or chicken and top with a layer of cheese.

Job 5:

Next, add the cucumber, then press the filling down slightly and top with the roll "lid".

Job 6:

The roll can be eaten immediately or wrapped in cling film and stored in the fridge for a few hours.

marks out of 10

10=yummylicious **9**=truly scrumptious
8=de-lovely **7**=delicious
6=tasty **5**=Mmmmmmm
4=mouth-watering **3**=just nice
2=good **1**=ok

. . . .

Poptastic ★★

Great fun to make and just as tasty
to eat, popcorn is the perfect snack!

Serves 4

prep: 5 minutes

cooking:
5 minutes

What you need:

1–2 tbsp vegetable oil
75g popping corn
1 tbsp butter
3 tbsp maple syrup
1 tbsp sesame seeds

Equipment:

• medium-sized saucepan with lid

• large mixing bowl

• small saucepan

• wooden spoon

Job 1: ❗

Pour the oil into a saucepan – it should cover the bottom of the pan. Heat the oil over a medium heat.

Job 2: ❗

Carefully add the popcorn to the pan in an even layer and cover with a lid; a glass lid is best so you can see into the pan.

Job 3: ❗

Cook the popcorn over a medium–low heat, shaking the pan occasionally, until the corn kernels pop.

Job 4: ❗

Pour the popcorn into a large mixing bowl, discarding any kernels that may not have popped.

Job 5: ❗

Melt the butter in a small saucepan, then pour in the maple syrup. Bring to the boil, then remove from the heat and cool.

Job 6: ❗

Pour the maple syrup sauce over the popcorn and add the sesame seeds; stir to mix together. Now you can tuck in!

marks out of 10

10=yummylicious 9=truly scrumptious
8=de-lovely 7=delicious
6=tasty 5=Mmmmmmm
4=mouth-watering 3=just nice
2=good 1=ok

. . . . ✓

29

Cinnamon raisin toast ★★

This delicious snack would also make a great breakfast served with yogurt and fruit or try as a pudding with your favourite ice cream. You could also use sliced bread, English muffins or brioche instead.

Serves 4

prep: 5 minutes

cooking: 10 minutes

What you need:

- 3 large eggs
- 8 tbsp milk
- 1 tsp ground cinnamon
- 2 tbsp caster sugar
- 1 tbsp sunflower oil
- 20g unsalted butter
- 4 slices raisin bread

Equipment:

- shallow dish
- fork or whisk
- large frying pan

Job 1:

Crack the eggs into a shallow dish and pour in the milk. Lightly beat with a fork or whisk until combined.

Job 2:

Next, add half the cinnamon and half the caster sugar to the egg mixture and stir or whisk until mixed in.

Job 3: !

Put half of the oil and butter in a large frying pan. Warm over a medium–low heat until the butter has melted.

Job 4: !

Swirl the butter and oil around the pan. Dip the raisin bread into the egg mixture until both sides are coated.

Job 5: !

Put two slices of the bread in the pan and cook for 2 minutes each side until golden. Keep warm.

Job 6: !

Heat the rest of the oil and butter in the pan and prepare and cook the rest of the raisin bread. Mix together the remaining caster sugar and cinnamon and sprinkle over the toast. Serve warm.

marks out of 10

10=yummylicious 9=truly scrumptious
8=de-lovely 7=delicious
6=tasty 5=Mmmmmmm
4=mouth-watering 3=just nice
2=good 1=ok

. . . . ✓

It's a wrap! ★★

These golden tortilla parcels are delicious as a light lunch served with vegetable sticks. They are filled with chopped tomato, tuna and melting mozzarella but you could also try pesto, cooked chicken or ham.

Serves 2

prep: 5 minutes

cooking:
4 minutes

What you need:

6 tbsp canned tuna, drained
2 soft flour tortillas
2 small tomatoes
8 slices mozzarella
2 tsp sunflower oil
salt and pepper

Equipment:

• small bowl
• fork
• sharp knife
• teaspoon
• chopping board
• frying pan
• spatula

Job 1:

Put the tuna in a bowl and mash with a fork. Spoon the tuna on to the centre of the tortillas.

Job 2: (!)

Halve the tomatoes, scoop out the seeds using a teaspoon, then throw away the seeds. Cut the tomatoes into small pieces.

Job 3:

Sprinkle the tomatoes on the tuna, then place the mozzarella on top. Season the filling with salt and pepper.

Job 4:

Carefully fold in the sides, then the ends of the tortillas to make 2 square-shaped parcels.

Job 5: (!)

Heat the oil in a frying pan and put the parcels in the pan, folded-side down.

Job 6: (!)

Cook the parcels for 4 minutes over a medium–low heat, turning once, until golden. Cut each diagonally in half before serving.

marks out of 10

10=yummylicious **9**=truly scrumptious
8=de-lovely **7**=delicious
6=tasty **5**=Mmmmmmm
4=mouth-watering **3**=just nice
2=good **1**=ok

. . . .

33

Cheese sticks ★★★

These golden cheese sticks are so good they just melt-in-the-mouth. They not only make a tasty after-school snack but are great party or picnic food, too.

Makes 16

prep: 10 minutes

cooking:
10 minutes

What you need:

100g plain flour, plus extra for
  dusting
½ tsp paprika (optional)
45g butter, plus extra for greasing
75g Parmesan cheese, finely grated
1 egg, lightly beaten

Equipment:

• 2 baking sheets
• sieve
• mixing bowl
• rolling pin
• wire cooling rack

Job 1: ❗

Turn the oven on to 200°C/400°F/Gas Mark 6. Lightly grease 2 baking sheets with butter.

Job 2:

Sift the flour and the paprika, if using, into a mixing bowl. Cut the butter into pieces, then add to the bowl.

Job 3:

Rub the butter into the flour with your fingertips until the mixture looks like breadcrumbs. Stir in the Parmesan cheese.

Job 4:

Stir the egg into the bowl with a fork, then use your hands to form the dough into a ball.

Job 5: ❗

Roll out the dough on a floured surface until 5mm thick. Trim the edges and cut into 16 x 1cm wide x 10cm long strips.

Job 6: ❗

Put the cheese sticks, spaced apart, on the baking sheets and cook for 10 minutes until golden. Cool on a wire rack.

marks out of 10

10=yummylicious 9=truly scrumptious
8=de-lovely 7=delicious
6=tasty 5=Mmmmmmm
4=mouth-watering 3=just nice
2=good 1=ok

. . . .

Meals in minutes

Treat your friends and family to these quick and simple ideas for lunch and dinner. There's something for everyone here with recipes influenced by dishes from different countries such as Italian spaghetti with meatballs, tasty Chinese noodles with chicken sticks and Mexican-style tortilla baskets filled with a lightly spiced bean stew.

Sunset soup ★★

This thick, golden-coloured soup would be great for a Halloween party – just the thing to warm you up on a cold Autumn night. You could also use pumpkin instead of the squash.

Serves 4

prep: 15 minutes

cooking:
30 minutes

What you need:

- 1 Kg butternut squash
- 1 tbsp olive oil
- 1 large onion, sliced
- 1 stick celery, sliced
- 1 leek, sliced
- 1 large carrot, sliced
- 1.2 litres vegetable stock
- 2 bay leaves
- 1 bouquet garni
- 1 tsp dried thyme
- Salt and pepper
- grated strong Cheddar cheese and crusty bread, to serve

Equipment:

- sharp Knife
- chopping board
- large saucepan with lid
- Spoon
- hand-held blender
- ladle
- grater

Job 1: ❗

Cut the squash into thick slices, then cut off the skin. Scoop out the seeds with a spoon and cut into chunks.

Job 2: ❗

Heat the oil in a saucepan and fry the onion for 5 minutes, then add the squash, celery, leek and carrot; stir well.

Job 3: ❗

Cook the vegetables for 3 minutes with the lid on. Pour in the stock and add the bay leaves, bouquet garni and thyme.

Job 4: ❗

Bring the soup to the boil, then reduce the heat and simmer, half covered, for 20 minutes until the vegetables are tender.

Job 5: ❗

Take the pan off the heat and, using an electric hand blender, whizz the soup until smooth. Season with salt and pepper.

Job 6: ❗

Ladle the soup into bowls and top with a sprinkling of grated cheese. Serve with crusty bread.

marks out of 10

10=yummylicious **9**=truly scrumptious
8=de-lovely **7**=delicious
6=tasty **5**=Mmmmmmm
4=mouth-watering **3**=just nice
2=good **1**=ok

. . . .

39

Salmon bites ★★

These golden, crispy balls of potato and brain-boosting salmon taste great and go well with the creamy dipping sauce.

Serves 4

prep: 20 minutes, plus chilling

cooking: 25 minutes

What you need:

2 x 213g cans salmon, skin and large bones removed

630g potatoes, peeled, cooked and cooled

1 small egg, beaten

flour, for coating

3 tbsp sunflower oil

salt and pepper

lemon wedges, to serve

Dipping sauce:

4 tbsp mayonnaise

2 tbsp tartare sauce

2 tbsp olive oil

1 tsp fresh lemon juice

Equipment:

• large mixing bowl

• grater

• spoon

• plate

• large frying pan

• spatula

• small mixing bowl

Job 1:

Put the salmon in a large bowl. Using your hands, flake the fish into chunks.

Job 2:

Grate the potatoes into the bowl with the salmon. Stir in the egg, salt and pepper. Cover the bowl and chill for 30 minutes.

Job 3:

Thickly cover a plate with flour. Take one spoonful of the salmon mixture at a time, about the size of a golf ball.

Job 4:

Using floured hands, shape the salmon mixture to make 16 balls, then dip each one in the flour until lightly coated.

Job 5: ❗

Heat the oil in a frying pan and fry half of the balls for 10 minutes, turning until golden. Repeat with the remaining balls.

Job 6:

Drain the balls on kitchen paper. Mix together the ingredients for the sauce, then serve with the salmon balls and lemon wedges.

marks out of 10

10=yummylicious **9**=truly scrumptious
8=de-lovely **7**=delicious
6=tasty **5**=Mmmmmmm
4=mouth-watering **3**=just nice
2=good **1**=ok

. . . .

41

Chicken sticks with oodles of noodles ★★

Fresh, fast and healthy, this recipe makes a perfect after-school supper to treat your friends and family.

serves 4

prep: 20 minutes, plus marinating

cooking: 15 minutes

What you need:

4 x 150g skinless chicken breasts, each one cut into 8 x 1cm cubes

250g medium egg noodles

2 spring onions, peeled and finely chopped

1 tbsp sesame seeds (optional)

Marinade:

4 tbsp soy sauce

2 tbsp toasted sesame oil

2 tbsp runny honey

5-cm piece fresh ginger, peeled and sliced

2 large cloves garlic, peeled and sliced

Equipment:

- shallow medium-sized dish
- sharp knife
- chopping board
- large spoon
- shallow dish
- cling film
- foil
- wooden skewers soaked in water until ready to use
- small and medium saucepans
- sieve

Job 1:

For the marinade, mix together the ingredients in a shallow dish. Add the chicken pieces and turn until coated; cover with cling film.

Job 2:

Chill, allowing the chicken to absorb the flavours of the marinade for at least 30 minutes, turning it occasionally.

Job 3: ❗

Turn on the grill to high, or heat a griddle. Thread the chicken pieces on to 8 wooden skewers, place in shallow dish and spoon over a little marinade.

Job 4: ❗

Grill or griddle the chicken sticks for 4 minutes. Turn the sticks over, spoon over more marinade, then cook for another 4 minutes.

Job 5: ❗

Cook the noodles following the packet instructions. Pour the marinade through a sieve into a small pan and boil gently for 1 minute, stirring.

Job 6:

To serve, put the noodles and skewers on to 4 plates. Spoon the marinade over the noodles and sprinkle with spring onions and sesame seeds (if using).

marks out of 10

10=yummylicious **9**=truly scrumptious
8=de-lovely **7**=delicious
6=tasty **5**=Mmmmmmm
4=mouth-watering **3**=just nice
2=good **1**=ok

. . . . ✔

Mighty meatball spaghetti ★★★

Everyone loves meatballs and these are no exception. They come in a rich tomato sauce and are served on a bed of swirly spaghetti. Sprinkle some extra grated Parmesan cheese over the meatballs if you like.

serves 4

prep: 20 minutes

cooking:
30 minutes

What you need:

45g crustless, day-old bread, broken into chunks
400g lean beef mince
2 cloves garlic, crushed
1 large egg, lightly beaten
40g Parmesan cheese, finely grated
flour, for coating
300g dried spaghetti
salt and pepper

Tomato sauce:

2 tbsp olive oil
2 cloves garlic, crushed
2 tsp dried oregano
2 x 400g cans chopped tomatoes
1 tbsp tomato purée
1 tsp sugar

Equipment:

• food processor

• 2 large saucepans, one with lid

• large spoon

• colander

Job 1: ⚠️

Put the bread in a food processor and whizz until it makes breadcrumbs. Add the mince, garlic, egg, Parmesan cheese, salt and pepper.

Job 2: ⚠️

Process the mince mixture until it comes together in a ball. Flour your hands and roll the mixture into balls the size of walnuts.

Job 3: ⚠️

Chill the balls, then make the tomato sauce. Heat the oil in a saucepan and add the garlic and oregano. Stir for 1 minute.

Job 4: ⚠️

Add the chopped tomatoes, tomato purée and sugar; bring to the boil, then reduce the heat and simmer for 8 minutes.

Job 5: ⚠️

Carefully place the meatballs in the pan and spoon the sauce over them. Cover and simmer for 20 minutes, turning the meatballs occasionally.

Job 6: ⚠️

Cook the pasta in a large pan of salted water, following the instructions on the packet. Drain and serve with the meatballs and sauce.

marks out of 10

10=yummylicious **9**=truly scrumptious
8=de-lovely **7**=delicious
6=tasty **5**=Mmmmmmm
4=mouth-watering **3**=just nice
2=good **1**=ok

. . . .

Mexican bean baskets ★★★

A tortilla makes the perfect basket shape when baked. Put a layer of crispy shredded lettuce in the basket if liked, then top with the bean stew. A spoonful of guacamole and grated cheese taste good, too.

Serves 4

prep: 15 minutes

cooking:
30 minutes

What you need:

2 tbsp olive oil, plus extra for brushing

2 onions, finely chopped

2 large cloves garlic, crushed

1 large red pepper, seeded and diced

2 courgettes, diced

3 tsp ground cumin

½ tsp ground cinnamon

2 tsp ground coriander

2 x 400g cans kidney beans, drained and rinsed

2 x 400g cans chopped tomatoes

2 tbsp tomato ketchup

4 large, soft tortillas

salt and pepper

Equipment:

• sharp knife

• chopping board

• large saucepan with lid

• pastry brush

• 4 heatproof bowls

• large baking sheet

Job 1: ❗

Turn the oven on to 180°C/350°F/Gas Mark 4. Heat the oil in a saucepan and add the onions. Stir to coat them in the oil.

Job 2: ❗

Cook the onions, with the lid on, for 8 minutes, stirring now and then. Stir in the garlic, red pepper and courgettes.

Job 3: ❗

Next, add the spices and kidney beans, followed by the tomatoes and ketchup. Bring to the boil, then reduce the heat.

Job 4: ❗

Half cover the pan with a lid and simmer for 20 minutes, stirring every now and then. Season with salt and pepper.

Job 5:

Lightly brush the tortillas on both sides with oil. Place each one in a heatproof bowl, shaping the sides to make a basket.

Job 6: ❗

Place the bowls on a baking tray and bake the tortillas for 9 minutes until crisp; leave to cool slightly and carefully remove from the bowls. Divide the beans between the "baskets".

marks out of 10

10=yummylicious **9**=truly scrumptious
8=de-lovely **7**=delicious
6=tasty **5**=Mmmmmmm
4=mouth-watering **3**=just nice
2=good **1**=ok

. . . .

Sweet treats

Your kitchen assistant won't need much persuading to join you in making these scrummy treats! You'll both have lots of fun preparing yummy puddings like the toffee banana sundae or delicious apple pie. Try making jam-filled cookies, decorating cupcakes with flowers and bugs or make your own sparkly chocolate truffles – they make the perfect gift!

Very berry big mess ★

Nothing could be simpler to make – or more delicious to eat – than this pudding with whipped vanilla cream, fresh strawberries and chunks of chocolate sponge.

Makes 4

prep: 15 minutes

cooking: none

What you need:

450g ripe strawberries, green part removed and halved or quartered

3 tbsp icing sugar

350ml whipping cream

2 tsp vanilla extract

4 slices chocolate sponge loaf or brownies

Equipment:

• electric blender

• sieve

• spoon

• small and large mixing bowls

• whisk or electric hand whisk

• wooden spoon

Job 1: (!)

Put 200g of the strawberries in a blender. Blend until puréed, then press through a sieve to remove any pips.

Job 2:

Put the rest of the strawberries in a bowl and sprinkle over 1 tbsp of the sugar. Stir and set aside.

Job 3: (!)

Pour the cream, the rest of the icing sugar and vanilla extract into a mixing bowl. Whisk the mixture until it forms soft peaks.

Job 4:

Break the sponge or brownies into large chunks and add to the cream with the strawberry purée.

Job 5:

Using a wooden spoon, gently stir the cake and strawberry purée into the whipped cream until it makes a ripple effect.

Job 6:

Spoon the cream mixture into 4 sundae dishes or bowls, then spoon over the rest of the strawberries and any juices.

marks out of 10

10=yummylicious 9=truly scrumptious
8=de-lovely 7=delicious
6=tasty 5=Mmmmmmm
4=mouth-watering 3=just nice
2=good 1=ok

. . . .

Toffee banana sundae ★★

There's only one way to describe this pudding…mmmmm! It's so delicious, it would make a great birthday treat – especially decorated with a chocolate flake or fudge stick.

Serves 3

prep: 15 minutes

cooking: 10 minutes

What you need:

140g golden syrup
2 tbsp caster sugar
2 tbsp soft light brown sugar
40g butter, cut into cubes
5 tbsp double cream
12 pecan nuts, halved (optional)
3 large bananas, peeled and sliced
9 scoops real dairy ice cream

Equipment:

- small saucepan
- wooden spoon
- frying pan
- ice cream scoop

Job 1:

Put the syrup, caster sugar, brown sugar and butter in the small saucepan. Stir to mix together and bring to the boil.

Job 2:

Let the syrup mixture bubble away for 5 minutes until slightly thickened, carefully stirring occasionally.

Job 3:

Leave the syrup mixture to cool slightly in the pan. Stir in the cream to make a toffee sauce.

Job 4:

Put the pecans in a dry frying pan and heat for 3 minutes until slightly toasted (if using). Set the nuts aside to cool.

Job 5:

Divide two thirds of the banana between 3 sundae dishes or bowls. Add 2 scoops of ice cream to each dish and a few pecans, if using.

Job 6:

Drizzle over a spoonful of the toffee sauce and top with another scoop of ice cream, the nuts, banana and some more sauce.

marks out of 10

10=yummylicious **9**=truly scrumptious
8=de-lovely **7**=delicious
6=tasty **5**=Mmmmmmm
4=mouth-watering **3**=just nice
2=good **1**=ok

. . . .

Chocolate sparkles ★★

These creamy milk chocolate truffles make the perfect gift: try presenting them in a cellophane bag, brightened up with a colourful ribbon, or a small gift box. Cake decorations make colourful coatings, so check out your favourites.

Makes about 5

prep: 25 minutes, plus chilling

cooking:
5 minutes

what you need:

300g good quality milk chocolate
100ml double cream
1 tsp vanilla extract
1 tbsp icing sugar
20g butter

To decorate:

hundreds and thousands; silver or
   pink stars; grated or flaked
   white chocolate, or your favourite
   colourful decorations

Equipment:

• heatproof mixing bowl

• medium-sized saucepan

• wooden spoon

• teaspoon

• oven gloves

• small paper cases

Job 1:

Break the chocolate into even-sized pieces and put it in a heatproof bowl with the cream.

Job 2: (!)

Put the bowl over a saucepan containing about 2.5cm of water – make sure the bowl rests on top and does not touch the water.

Job 3: (!)

Heat the water – but do not let it boil – and gently melt the chocolate, stirring occasionally to mix it with the cream.

Job 4: (!)

Using oven gloves, remove the bowl from the pan and leave to cool slightly. Stir in the vanilla extract, icing sugar and butter until mixed in.

Job 5:

Chill until the mixture firms up. Use a teaspoon to scoop up some of the mixture, then roll into a ball shape. Repeat until the mixture is used up.

Job 6:

Dip the chocolate balls into your favourite coatings, turning them until they are evenly coated. Arrange the chocolates in small paper cases.

marks out of 10

10=yummylicious **9**=truly scrumptious
8=de-lovely **7**=delicious
6=tasty **5**=Mmmmmmm
4=mouth-watering **3**=just nice
2=good **1**=ok

. . . . ✔

Flower and bug cupcakes ★★

Making and decorating your own cupcakes is such fun. Experiment with different coloured icing and cake decorations to create your own versions of these flower and bug cakes.

Makes 12

prep: 10 minutes

cooking: 15–20 minutes

what you need:

175g self-raising flour
1 tsp baking powder
175g caster sugar
175g very soft unsalted butter, cut into small pieces
3 eggs at room temperature
1 tsp vanilla extract
2 tbsp milk

Decoration:

200g icing sugar
1 tbsp lemon juice
1–2 tbsp water
few drops of blue and green food colouring
white chocolate buttons
white chocolate rainbow buttons
jelly bug sweets

Equipment:

• large paper or plastic cases
• bun tin
• large mixing bowl
• electric hand mixer
• wooden spoon
• metal spoons
• wire cooling rack

Job 1:

Turn the oven on to 180°C/350°F/Gas Mark 4. Put 12 paper cases into a bun tin. Sift the flour, baking powder and caster sugar into a bowl.

Job 2:

Next, add the butter, eggs, vanilla extract and milk. Use an electric hand mixer or wooden spoon to make a smooth, creamy mixture.

Job 3:

Divide the cake mixture between the paper cases. Bake for 15–20 minutes until risen and golden. Cool on a wire rack.

Job 4:

Mix together the icing sugar, lemon juice and water to make a smooth icing. Colour half of the icing blue and half of the icing green.

Job 5:

Spread the icing over the cakes. For flower cakes, place a white chocolate button in the centre and the rainbow ones around it.

Job 6:

For bug cakes, pipe a leaf or blades of grass using the green icing on each cake and top with a jelly bug.

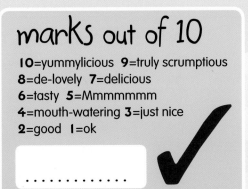

marks out of 10

10=yummylicious **9**=truly scrumptious
8=de-lovely **7**=delicious
6=tasty **5**=Mmmmmmm
4=mouth-watering **3**=just nice
2=good **1**=ok

. . . . ✔

Jammy drops ★★

These golden, buttery, vanilla biscuits taste similar to shortbread but have a delicious gooey jam centre. Share them with your family and friends for a teatime treat.

Makes 15

prep: 15 minutes, plus chilling

cooking: 12 minutes

What you need:

- 100g softened unsalted butter, cut into small pieces
- 5 tbsp caster sugar
- 1 egg, lightly beaten
- 1 tsp vanilla extract
- 135g self-raising flour
- 4 tbsp cornflour
- 4 tsp strawberry jam

Equipment:

- large mixing bowl
- electric hand mixer
- wooden spoon
- small bowl
- sieve
- 2 baking sheets
- baking paper
- tablespoon

Job 1:

Put the butter and caster sugar into a mixing bowl. Whisk with an electric mixer or beat with a wooden spoon until light and creamy.

Job 2:

Mix together the egg and vanilla extract and add, a little at a time, to the bowl, whisking or beating until mixed in.

Job 3:

Next, sift the flour and cornflour into the bowl and gently fold in with a wooden spoon to make a fairly soft dough.

Job 4:

Turn on the oven to 180°C/350°F/Gas Mark 4. Line 2 baking sheets with baking paper to prevent the biscuits sticking.

Job 5:

Take a heaped tablespoon of the mixture and form it into a ball. Repeat to make 15 balls and place them spaced apart on the baking sheet.

Job 6:

Chill the biscuits for 15 minutes, then use your thumb to make an indent in the middle and fill with jam. Bake for 12 minutes.

marks out of 10

10=yummylicious **9**=truly scrumptious
8=de-lovely **7**=delicious
6=tasty **5**=Mmmmmmm
4=mouth-watering **3**=just nice
2=good **1**=ok

. . . .

My own apple pie ★★★

To make your personalised apple pies, roll out the pastry and carefully cut out your initials, and those of your family. After brushing the pies with egg, stick on the letters and brush again before baking.

Makes 4

prep: 20 minutes, plus chilling

cooking: 30–35 minutes

what you need:

225g plain flour
pinch of salt
2 tbsp icing sugar
120g cold unsalted butter
  (or half butter and half vegetable
  fat), cut into small pieces
1 egg, separated
1–2 tbsp cold water

Filling:

675g eating apples, peeled, halved,
  cored and thinly sliced
2 tbsp orange juice
1 tsp ground cinnamon
3 tbsp caster sugar

Equipment:

• large mixing bowl

• 4 x 200ml small heatproof dishes

• rolling pin

• baking sheet

• sharp knife

Job 1:

Sift the flour, salt and icing sugar into a bowl. Add the butter and rub it into the flour mixture with your fingertips.

Job 2:

When the mixture looks like fine breadcrumbs, mix in the egg yolk and water. Form the mixture into a ball with your hands.

Job 3:

Cover the pastry dough with clingfilm and chill for 30 minutes. Mix the apple with the orange juice, cinnamon and caster sugar.

Job 4: (!)

Turn on the oven to 200°C/400°F/Gas Mark 6. Divide the apple mixture between the 4 heatproof dishes. Wet the rim of each dish.

Job 5: (!)

Roll out the pastry and cut 4 round tops. Top each pie with a pastry round, trim the edges and crimp with a fork.

Job 6: (!)

Brush each pie with egg white and make a slit in the top; decorate as described on page 60. Put on a baking sheet and bake for 30–35 minutes.

marks out of 10

10=yummylicious **9**=truly scrumptious
8=de-lovely **7**=delicious
6=tasty **5**=Mmmmmmm
4=mouth-watering **3**=just nice
2=good **1**=ok

. . . .

Cooking words

Here are some cookery terms that you will find in this book with simple explanations:

Bake: cook a food/dish in the oven.

Beat: stir or mix an ingredient in order to add air.

Blend: mix ingredients together in a food processor or blender to make a smooth mixture or liquid.

Boil: heat a liquid, such as water, over a high heat until it bubbles.

Chill: cool an ingredient or food in the refrigerator.

Chop: cut an ingredient into smaller pieces.

Cream: beat butter and sugar together using a wooden spoon or food processor to add air until it is light and fluffy.

Drain: pour off unwanted liquid, sometimes through a colander or sieve, or remove excess oil after frying by placing the food on kitchen paper.

Drizzle: slowly pour a trickle of a liquid or sauce over a food.

Dry-fry: cook ingredients, such as nuts and seeds, in a frying pan without oil.

Fold in: mix one ingredient into another but gently, and sometimes gradually, to prevent losing any air.

Fry: cook food in oil in a frying pan or saucepan over a direct heat.

Grate: rub food, such as cheese, vegetables or chocolate, up and down a grater over holes of varying sizes to make thin or thick shreds.

Grease: lightly coat a baking sheet, cake tin or dish using oil or butter to prevent sticking.

Grill: cook or brown food under intense heat.

Juice: extract liquid from an ingredient, such as fruit, using a squeezer or an electric juicer.

Marinade: a mixture of oil, herbs, spices and other flavourings used to flavour a food such as meat and fish, before cooking.

Marinate: flavour an ingredient, such as meat or fish, by soaking it in a mixture of oil, herbs, spices and other flavourings for a period of time.

Mash: crush food, such as bananas or cooked potatoes, to give a smooth end result.

Melt: turn a solid, such as chocolate or butter, into a liquid, using heat.

Peel: remove the skin from food, such as fruit and vegetables, using a peeler or small knife.

Purée: blend or liquidize (usually with a little water) a food, such as fruit or vegetables, into a pulp.

Rinse: place food under a cold running water tap.

Roll out: flatten a food, such as pastry, into a smooth, even layer using a rolling pin.

Roughly chop: cut an ingredient into pieces of varying sizes.

Rub in: mix fat, such as butter, into flour with your fingertips until the mixture looks like fine breadcrumbs.

Season: add flavour to food using salt and pepper.

Sift: put an ingredient, such as flour, through a sieve to remove lumps and add air.

Simmer: cook food gently in a pan over a low direct heat, making sure it does not boil.

Slice: cut a food into thick or thin strips/pieces.

Stir: mix ingredients together to combine them into one mixture and prevent sticking if being cooked.

Whisk: quickly stir or mix an ingredient or mixture, using a fork or a kitchen utensil called a whisk, in order to add air.

Index

almonds 18
apple pie 60
apples 16, 60

bacon 22
bananas 14, 52
beef mince 44
breakfasts
    Big breakfast 22
    Cinnamon apple
        purée 16
    Flipping good 20
    Going bananas 14
    Golden nuggets 18
    Perfect porridge 16
    Sunrise crush 14
butternut squash 38

cake decorations 54, 56
carrots 38
celery 38
cheese 26
    Cheddar 38
    mozzarella 32
    Parmesan 34, 44
chicken 26, 42
chocolate 54
cleanliness 5
coconut milk 14
corn, popping 28
courgettes 46
cream 50, 52, 54
cucumber 26
cupcakes 56

egg noodles 42
eggs 20, 22, 30, 34, 40, 44,
    56, 58, 60

ginger 42
golden syrup 52

ham 26
honey 18, 42

ice cream 52

kidney beans 46

leeks 38
lettuce 26

mangoes 14
maple syrup 16, 20, 28

oranges 14

pancakes 20
pecan nuts 16, 52
peppers, red, 46
pesto 26
pineapples 14
porridge oats, 16, 18
potatoes 22, 40

quick meals
    Chicken sticks with
        oodles of noodles 42
    Mexican bean
        baskets 46
    Mighty meatball
        spaghetti 44
    Salmon bites 40
    Sunset soup 38

raisins 18
raspberries 18

safety 5
salmon 40
seeds 18, 28, 42
snacks
    Cheese sticks 34
    Cinnamon raisin toast 30
    It's a wrap! 32
    Poptastic 28
    Roll up, roll up! 26
soup 38
soy sauce 42
spaghetti 44
spring onions 42
strawberries 50
strawberry jam 58
summer fruits 20
sweet dishes
    Chocolate sparkles 54
    Flower and bug
        cupcakes 56
    Jammy drops 58
    My own apple pie 60
    Toffee banana
        sundae 52
    Very berry big mess 50

techniques 6
tomato purée 44
tomatoes 32
    canned 44, 46
    cherry 22
tortillas 32, 46
tuna 32

walnuts 18

yogurt 14, 20